To Brother Phil,

Thank you for taken the time to help me reach my dream. When I was lost to find someone to keep the face of my passion. You came and show an amazing hand to give my second book a face. I'm truly thankful that you gave a Helping hand. You will forever be a brother that I will pray for and hope in the future God give you a clear future to what your goals may take you. Thank you

Desert Rose

Desert Rose

Words for Thoughts

By Sheka Mansaray

Copyright © 2009 by Sheka Mansaray.

Library of Congress Control Number: 2009912226
ISBN: Hardcover   978-1-4415-7891-4
               Softcover   978-1-4415-7890-7

All rights reserved. No part of this book may be reproduced or transmitted in any form or by any means, electronic or mechanical, including photocopying, recording, or by any information storage and retrieval system, without permission in writing from the copyright owner.

This book was printed in the United States of America.

To order additional copies of this book, contact:
Xlibris Corporation
1-888-795-4274
www.Xlibris.com
Orders@Xlibris.com
72071

CONTENTS

Acknowlegments 11

Envious 15
Us all 16
Gone 19
Worthy 20
Youth 21
To see you 23
Brown Sugar 24
Natural 25
Night in Africa 26
Win 27
Midnight 28
Heart jumping 29
Glance to Fame 30
Burning Art 31
Black Thorn 32
Beholder 33
Scars My Soul 34
Secrets 35
Brown Beauty 36
"yes" 37
2030 38
Reality 39
We are Africans 40
Words For Thoughts 42
Heartless Soul 43
Liquid Thoughts 44

Dead Man Grave	45
If Be	46
My Star	47
Honor	48
Last Wisdom	49
Star	50
Sallie	51
Accident	52
Innocent	53
Deal to Wrong	54
Gloomy	55
Desert Rose	56
Strength	57
Inferno	59
Hate	60
No to Truth	61
I Know Love	62
Glory Be To Man	63
Smiling	64
Words Holding	65
Dry Your Eyes	67
To My Knees	68
Summer Love	70
Divine	71
Lie's	72
The Rebirth of Africa	73
Unselfish	75
Photograph	76
The Dream	77
Poetry	78

This book is inspired and dedicated
To the people of my heart
and the hero's of my soul.

Sweet desert rose
This memory of Eden haunts us all
This desert flower
This rare perfume, is the sweet intoxication of the fall.

—Sting and *Cheb Mami*, "Desert Rose"

Acknowlegments

I would like to express my gratitude to all the talented and amazing individuals who gave me the possibility and contributions at various stages to complete this book.

Thank you to Sarah Thorson for her hard work put in to my first and second book to create my dream.

Thank you to Kristen Erickson for guiding me along my journey and helping me polish my dream with your wonderful insight for what I needed to work on in my book.

With a special thanks to Wally Agboola for his talented photographys taken of me for my first and second book.

Also I would like to give thanks to Phillip Wiltzius for creating the cover of this book. Keep your amazing talent going may you be blessed with a great future to come.

To my friends and family and to those who I did not mention thanks for giving me the courage to stand up on my own. My dream would have never happened without you lending me your hearts and shoulders to lean on.

The real hero of this book woud be God. Lord thank you for blessing me with my gift and wonderful people in my life.

Corinthians 9:15—"Thanks be to God for his indescribable gift!,"

Psalm 30:12—"That my heart may sing to you and not be silent. O Lord my God, I will give you thanks for ever."

Years ago,

When I was a young boy I remember the way my Grandmother used to converse with me; filling my head with pictures, parables and poetry. My Grandmother was never one to just hand an answer to me. Instead, she would wrap them within a story to delight and satisfy my then cheerful spirit. My thoughts feel deeper in the memory of her stories, and the truth within her parables.

Right about now I'm sure you're wondering what this is all about. This is about the heart and the soul. This is my letter, or perhaps my lessons learned from the past, to share with all of you. I trust the poems that are within this book will help you understand what the heart and soul mean to me. I have plunged deeply into the thoughts and feelings of those around me hoping to gain a better understanding behind the meaning of the words heart and soul. I've been taught that the heart is a hollow, muscular organ. That by its rhythmic contraction acts as a force to maintain the circulation of blood that keeps us alive. I've learned that in a literary, emotional sense it is the repository of one's deepest and most sincere feelings. The heart represents our intellect and our imagination; but it is also our strength, our will, and our determination. And when necessary, can make us do and say unpleasant things.

The soul, to me, is akin to the relationship you have with yourself. Your soul grows and learns with you, as naturally as breathing, to encompass all that you experience. In this context the soul contains an inestimable amount of value. Our soul contains our love, our courage, our Spirit. It shows itself in our characteristics, our fire, our Energy, our fervor, our affection, and ardor; all noble manifestations of the soul. I also believe that the inherent power of our kindness is held deep within our soul. We can share with others the beauty or the ugliness of our soul.

What I have come to realize about the nature of the heart and the belief in the soul came through the creation of this book; *Desert Rose: Words for Thoughts*. Perhaps, through the poems I have plowed and sowed from my heart and soul, I can impart theses realizations to you. William Convino said "Body and soul speak two languages, which are not only different, even inconsistent, but also inaudible to each other. The inner sense alone is able to hear and comprehend them both, also having the role of translating one into the other" (*History of Phantasy* by William A Covino). I hope the two languages will translate harmoniously as you allow each of these poems to sink into your heart and comfort your soul. Welcome to *Desert Rose: Words for Thoughts*.

Envious

When your life no longer finds you intelligent,
Race not to your wrongs to define the purpose of your being.
Look deep within to find the integrity of your heart,
to keep you running on life's path.
Be not afraid, for fear's eyes only Stare
Upon you as weakness. You must know to
Fight fear with intensity, hope and love.
Be not jumbled, for life's journey is filled with envy,
suspicions and vigilance that you must overcome through
The tenderness of your wisdom.
When life no longer finds you intelligent,
Reach not to your wrongs to define the purpose of your being.

Us all

I'm that hope which is brought to us all
I'm the wisdom of your future and the pain of your past
I'm the mystery in life lying under the thoughts of history.
I'm insanity, I speak with a spark called creativity,
Who am I?
I'm that hope which is brought to us all
I'm a man of loss,
pain and hope buried under the thoughts of disappointment.
I'm the voice that never speaks,
my actions stand alone with my shadow.
I'm hope's words and freedom's hands,
I feel the changes of my past shining for my future.
Who am I?
I'm the warrior that could not fall under the whips of slavery,
I'm the sun's thought and the moon's son.
Look no further
I'm here to paint the world with my blessing.
I'm here
I come strong and bright like the sun's painting.
Who am I? . . . you already know.

Stay with me here, please, on this journey.

A close friend was walking towards a path to find forever.

Now, I know what you're thinking. Please, stay with me. Please, keep reading.

I think that forever is insanely overrated. It is though, isn't it? I mean, your loved one says to you "I will love you forever" and then you break-up or get divorced; the anger within holds you. A sharp pain, like needles to your arm or a million burns to the chest, breaks out from inside of you and releases the hurt from within. Though you may still love them that love cannot be forever once evil comes between you. I wonder if you've ever thought clearly about this. What does forever really mean? Where does it come from? Is it real?

Please, stay with me on this journey . . . .

A close friend was walking towards a path to finding forever. Just when he believed his life was endless he was reminded of how nothing ever lasts forever. He'd seen others fall down and never get back up. He'd seen heroes, leaders and champions fall. He walks to find the meaning of forever. One night he says to me, "I need someone to put my heart back together". I replied, "What can I do?"

There have been those who have a strong enough heart to help others. He says, "Whose heart is strong enough to put a million pieces of a shattered heart together? I long to see their face to save me from this world so I can find a forever free from pain, sadness, sorrow and heartbreak".

We may never really know how long forever is going to be for each of us. Within the pain everyone's forever is different. Your life, for you, is forever. Unfortunately there is death, and in a way that is how life goes on. Really, have you ever sat and thought about a family member that is not near you. They are hoping in their heart and deep within the roots of their soul that they will see you again. Eleven years have passed since I last saw my family. I hope with all my heart and deep into my soul that I will see them again soon. That is what forever feels like to me.

So what is this forever that those who are in love, or those that believe they know the truth talk about? Who are we as humans to define love, truth and forever? You may say that you are in love. You may say that you will forever keep truth in your heart. You may wish on shooting stars. But really no one knows. You may love for a day or a hundred years but once it ends your forever is forever no more.

I suppose, much like my friend, we may never truly find forever. But see past my words, they are my thoughts and perhaps my thoughts alone. But I believe that forever only lasts so long. Maybe forever is overrated. Where does forever come from? How long is it really?

Gone

My mind is gone.
The thoughts of yesterday bring
The light that awaits to transform my soul.
Gone to find faith, nevertheless to find the heart is no longer the soul's partner.
My mind is gone, finding that
challenges come to brawl with insanity.
Hoping and wishing are fixations that alter paths.
My mind has gone away with the thoughts of yesterday,
Gone to witness life within an hour,
every moment formed of minutes,
every minute made of seconds,
every second becoming a dream, to which reality is distorted.
My mind has gone away with the thoughts of yesterday,
Gone to raising the sky with love, giving the moonlight a joy to remember.
If rain is the sky, what is tears to the eye?
My mind has gone away with the thoughts of yesterday,
Gone to see where pain kisses it with sorrow,
and development of the future is left to rot.
How can love find you?
I confessed to the truth, spoken from my own tongue,
Expressing the beauty among my soul and heart
My mind is gone, along with the thoughts of yesterday,
Gone to witness life within an hour,
every moment formed of minutes,
every minute made of seconds,
every second becoming a dream, to which reality is distorted.

Worthy

Beauty starts with truth which encourages
your smile
So worthy you are
Your beauty is my truth and my style.
In your eyes I see a vision of a perfect dream.
A dream that can be painted with just us two
A thought that holds the stillness of faith
Your smile takes me higher, like a child with new wisdom.
A worthy dream unlocks my interests
I fall into the sunlight of your kisses full of joy,
Beauty starts with truth which encourages your smile
So worthy you are
Your beauty is my truth and my style.

Youth

The rise in gun crime
Is bathing the news in blood.
Our children need to be protected,
that's why they carry knives and guns.
We, the grown-ups, have failed in doing our job.
The experts' words fall
on deaf ears. In our youth gained blood bath,
another teenager goes down,
another teenager gunned down .
Don't watch the news,
they know. They see anger through
scars on arms, cuts and bruises
from fists hitting flesh, as well as knuckles on belts.
The city has a different kind of darkness,
it falls under the golden veins of life and death.
Another teenager goes down,
another teenager gunned down.
The city has a different kind of darkness.
It falls in layers of black confusion,
Swallowing the youth whole, eating into
the streets' unwritten codes.

Dying from a single bullet wound to the chest,
another teenager goes down,
another teenager gunned down.
Cough out the truth and watch death become a freedom
The crime scene is witnessed by the random
street-light. The blood stains are small, but fatal.
Another teenager goes down,
another teenager gunned down.
The expert continues.
Panic rises in guilty echoes, scenes of
wild dogs' and their desperate barks to match
The sound of footsteps, running.
The rise in knife crime
is bathing the news in blood.
Our children need to be protected,
another teenager goes down,
another teenager gunned down.

To see you

Every night I fly away
In tears, to sleep.
In every dream I am foretold
of the day we'll meet.
Here I go again.
Tell me what it takes to see you.
I would leave it all to see you,
I would leave it all to find you.
Will we meet again?
Will I see you again?
Will we be joined forever,
will we stand side by side together?
Your light has died,
your kiss has gone and dried up.
Your eyes, so cold; yet empty.
You have gone, where are you?
How I yearn for you,
how I want to be there,
where you are?
To feel your touch, and hear your words,
No matter how far.
Will I see you again?
We will meet again?
We will be joined forever,
standing side by side together?

Brown Sugar

The moon and the stars shine because your words hold truth.
Your smile brightens the daybreak.
Oh so wonderful,
oh so beautiful.
What can one say to a soul so true?
Won't you come and show me the truth?
My brown sugar
You give love that shines our path.
You are my eyes,
my freedom and devotion.
Be lonely no more.
Be loved always.
Your lips speak of my game, while
keeping truth in my name.
My brown sugar
Won't you come into the dark with me?
Come play my game and take my last name,
Be not afraid nor ashamed
Won't you come and play my game
Come in and see what your mind can win,
My love is sweet, never a sin.
My brown sugar
See, the moon and the stars shine because your words hold truths
Wont you come into the dark and show me the truths
My brown sugar
Don't lie with the truth in your heart.
Let me make you scream, clenching what you desire, your mind can win,
I promise it is good for your soul, never a sin
Won't you come into the dark with me and show me your truths?

Natural

Oh there she is, lovely as can be.
Oh there she is, sweet as a bee.
Her eyes, oh so true and oh so natural.
When she smiles and speaks,
her words sing to my soul.
There she goes,
there she be,
looking lovely just for me.
Oh there she is, lovely as can be.
Oh there she is, sweet as a bee.
Live no more in fear my queen,
for I'm here as your king.
If there be forever love,
Forever love she shall be
Her smile warm and free.
She feeds my mind and hugs my soul.
Oh there she is, lovely as can be.
Oh there she is, sweet as a bee.
She leaves my heart jumping,
wanting for more.
Oh lord let my mind hold her curves.
For I'm the truth and the one she deserves.
For I'm her man-to-be and serve
Oh lord release the words within
For her I lust, I have sinned
Oh there she is, lovely as can be.
Oh there she is, sweet as a bee.

Night in Africa

Last sunrise, I dreamt of a night in Africa.
A dream that came with both sadness and tears of happiness.
I watched my thoughts in Zambia's Victoria Falls and I realized the soft wind from the north came grasping for me to take action.
Breaths of fresh air I inhale.
Freedom escapes from my lungs as it matches the drifting of my boat.
I ride smoothly as I glide my fingers down to grab the reflection of the country soul.
Last sunrise, I dreamt of a night in Africa
The palm trees await freely.
I, myself, awakened in the slave kingdom of Ghana,
I felt the pain of my heroes and I embraced their light.
I gather my hands and gain a cooling refreshment of the Nile River.
I give thanks for a new day.
Last sunrise, I had a dreamt of a night in Africa
Timeless journey came, I walked in footsteps of languages that embrace my soul.
I walked in the desert and found my hero's footsteps waiting to match my own.
I saw their inspiration sinking deep in my thoughts and created a future for my wisdom.
I saw the sun going down, with peace lying on its back.
Saying good night, except
to find hours awaken, good morning.
I had a dream of a night in Africa.

Win

There was a reflection that glided through my memory.
She's my soul.
Moments spent with her I see God within.
She's my dream and my goal is her love to win.
She's my thoughts, my books and my pen.
She holds the truth in my life; I do the best I can.
She waits for my last name,
a day that marks smiles and gladness; never provocation or shame.
Moments spent with her I see God within
She's my dream and my goal is her love to win.
I'm her love and her love is my star, when she smiles I shine.
There are times I get lost in her eyes and find myself in her heart.
A bond of closeness, never parted.
Moments spent with her I see God within.
She's my dream and my goal is her love to win.
She's my heart my soul, jealousy you will not find bottled within
She is the sweetest soul, you will not find her be a supporter of sin.
Her comfort is within freedom songs,
songs that keep me on path to never do wrong.
There is no other beauty that stands, only one.
She signifies memories of unforgettable passion.
Moments spent with her I see God within
She's my dream and my goal is her love to win
She feeds me knowledge that birth a new wisdom
She's the truth, the faith, and the kingdom
Moments spend with her I see God within.

Midnight

It was a midnight in November.
She spoke to me saying, "I got too much into drinking one summer ago."
With shame floating in her eyes she continues,
"Alcoholism and drug abuse runs in my family with uncles and cousins,
you see, I'm trying to stay away from sins."
As questions passed and clouds hold hands with time, she asked,
"Why are you such a nice guy?
And how come you don't already have a girlfriend,
if you are so sweet and handsome?" He replies with a sense of heart broken.
Whispers pass pictures that came to haunt him with his answer saying
"I don't know. I guess sometime it's about dreams and goals and some
don't see that,
I mean I need love and love don't need me, what to do?"
His heart held still, like a favorite song on pause.
Out of anger, a moment gave confidence to her will, she said,
"It just sucks. I want to find that guy who really loves me
we can have great communication, He has to have
sense of humor, trusting and truth in him, you know?
someone who wants to work through problems and not throw
everything away over small shit."
She looked deeply into his hopeless eyes and found his heart crying for
help. She said, "You understand what I'm trying to say right?
A set of soft breath passes and he sighed "to be honest with you, I
don't even know any more."
She looked at him while visions of her love stood still, waiting for a love
that holds trust and truth.

Heart jumping

I can see your heart jumping out for me.
I can feel your pain screaming out for me.
I can't do this,
I won't do this.
I can see your heart jumping out for me.
I can see your tears falling for me.
How can I do this?
How can we do this?
I can feel your pain screaming out for me.
There is no need to hide,
the truth is out, the blame is on my side.
Can we see the seeds of hope in our eyes?
Can we see the question that has no why?
I can feel your pain screaming out for me.
I have undressed the pain and lies.
I can see your tears staining my memories.
I can't do this,
I won't do this.

Glance to Fame

She's singing for my soul. Her lyricism becomes medicine that
my tender heart craves.
Her poetry is the soft wind from the north,
a beautiful blues song from the south, and
the sweetest breath. She's the beauty that shines within my heart.
She has elegance in her voice, and her style paints her steps of grace.
Double-sided mirrors are reflections of her past, and show her future
with a clearer glance to fame.

Burning Art

Will there be cries heard as I
burn art?
Flying into the sunset,
ashes flicker, the sky turns black.
Will there be cries heard as I
burn art?
I cry, lonely in your inner hot core.
Flying into the sunset,
away in the empty sky,
will there be cries heard as I
burn art?
Flying into the sunset.
Staring until the sky turns blank.
Like the memories of a child's dreams,
the soul speaks. Minds lead,
intelligence cries. Heart dies.
Will there be cries heard as I
burn art?

Black Thorn

Last morning I saw a rose; soft, bright and red.
Black thorn, beautiful rose.
No pain, nor does it have sorrow.
This rose's heart is clean, clear and never complains.
I saw a rose awake.
Last morning a rose smell as sweet like cocoa brown,
always welcoming, delightful and fresh like morning dew.
I saw a rose last morning, oh, what a beautiful morning.
I saw a rose awake.

Beholder

Beauty is in the eyes of the beholder.
Beauty is in the mind and the soul.
Beauty is in the words that she speaks.
Beauty is in her heart, so it's never cold.
I lengthening the sense of her warmth against mine.
To share a level of intimacy that only we can speak,
I cannot discontinue this lust
Wanting to bury my passion
Wanting to let her explore my cadaver
Wanting to let her be my comforter
Wanting to tell her everything
from one corner to another
Beauty in the eyes of the beholder.
Beauty in the mind and the soul.
Beauty in the words that she speaks.
Beauty in her heart, so it's never cold.
I wish I could enfold my arms around her.
I wish I could experience her lips on mine.
I wish this lust wasn't so strapping.
Beauty in her heart, so it's never cold.
Beauty in the words that she speaks.
Beauty in her mind and her soul.

Scars My Soul

The affliction that is so, scars my soul.
Rooted in those evil feelings of personal inadequacy,
how have I come to resent what another presents? As if I have never been a candidate for representation, only I can choose.
Hateful waters run deep.
What is funny is that it very truly could not exist if there were genuine equality amongst all, there I go again, dreaming. Unfortunately a dream that is probably worth the wait,
Is there no cure for such an acute illness, if it be so then let so be it for the sake of my survival, So I let universal equality flood the globe, bring forth the global inner peace and love that can only lead to the peace that lays jealousy on her back,
I find myself suffering her symptoms, on bended knee a question, a glance, open my mind should I call with a genuine need to appreciate a fellow man's fortune ? Because wishing fortune upon another can only increase your peace, whereas praying for another's misfortune will only assist you in your own missed fortune,
It is eternally good to rejoice in man's achievements, whether they be mine, yours, or his, in the end they are all ours, The call must be said that each man represents all man in the midst of equality, I must admit I have had my time of honor and wickedness as to what other should have or have not.
I have given all that I had as those have given to me. As we all know our own lives the water sometimes falls on our waterfalls we cannot lose sight of what it means to be alive, So I fight the feeling to act out of spite, because for every plight there is a brilliant light that shines on, and on and on it shines, on yours and mine, and the means will be revealed in time to the affliction that is so scars my soul.

Secrets

Bring your mind to my secrets but not with words.
I'll show you a special places but only in darkness.
Pain will be our joy as well as our laughter's.
Be not afraid
the storm of our passion will bliss
the beats of our hearts
draw near
heair
the sound of joy plays with smiles.
When the sky lit up with your smile
we will dance to my secrets and awaken the beauty that others don't see.
Your bright wisdom will give everlasting life to the cliffs,and the
mountains, which you have given me,
bring your mind to my secrets but not with words.
I'll show you a special places but only in darkness.
Pain will be our joy as well as our laughter's.

Brown Beauty

Beauty, brown
woman
Gifted with culture and strength
Her wisdom never stain thoughts, always bright
Gifted with spritual light
Touch by the smoothness of the sun
Peaceful dreams came with acceptance of memories,
Gifted with peace of the night
Brown beauty
Beauty brown
woman
Gifted with culture and strength
Growths in faith to find comfort
soft breath echoes as another lay in loyalty
Gifted with spiritual light
Young mind assemble free as puzzle parts
peace on a journey with strong faith
Brown beauty
Beauty, brown
woman
Gifted with truth from the heart
lost in her conscious of daydreaming;
introduced by comfort in her eyes,
Manifesting her truth,
discover my name written in her heart,
Brown beauty
Beauty, brown
woman

"yes"

All she said that night was
"yes"
Time passes, clouds became gloom
Fantasies that once stood shy refuse to be Expired.
give up the ghost
became a possibility for reality
Questions linger to exacted foreplay with undone breathes saying
"yes"
All there is to be came to existense
All the dying passion sinks with melted thoughts and wild whispers
says good night and hello says good bye
All she said is "yes".

2030

When the moon fell to earth
It was on that day I saw men became life's children,
wildness and mindless for their actions,
on that very day children became heroes,
mother smiles as father hold their name as noble call.
I saw smiles that were held up for decades find peace with crumb dust and sadness.
The sorrow came upon me as I fixed my hands upon my face afraid to see what had become of my time.
I felt that I was frozen in a vision that of which lighting struck.
I was scared awake to a cold and dusty cloud.
I saw Daylight giving birth to darkness,
each scream roamed as I waited with visions half full and half bluer.
I heard angels and demons plotting with philosophers and poets,
from every household and to every street corner, thieves found joy,
momentarily, only to find death holding their path,
young girls fight, victims of rape, and homeless men and women find safety; the poor mans gift.
I saw all faiths fight for freedom to feed one cause which liberates the mind and helps one another.
When the moon fell to earth

Reality

What is this reality of ours?
It is the question that I ask
If need be bless,
Please bless me
And confined a sense of reality in my mind
I find this reality a dream
And my dream
Is now my reality.

We are Africans

Let us say it with no shame
We are loved and hated by strangers
Who find our people to be all the same
Our mother's heart beats
For our human race
Her love overtakes our minds and dances with our souls
We are fathers, mothers, heroes and legends
We are Africans
The shape of our
Mountains, streams and rivers
The richness of our lands,
The beautiful complexion of our women in East Africa,
West Africa,
Central Africa
And South Africa
Beautiful and strong
Black is who we are, not our soul
Times have fed our sisters and brothers with poverty and H.I.V.

We are Africans
We are here today to honor our mother Africa
We are here to show her we care
We're here to show her that we know where we came from
Our ancestors left us with pride and education to define Knowledge
Destroyed not our people's pride,
For such a gift is needed in our heart
We are Africans
Let us say it with no shame
The heavy hanging changes of life's ways
Will fall and the sun will illuminate
Our starting path
Our forefathers have swept our path clean
With the broom of peace, wisdom and love
To love our self and our people
We are Africans
Let us say it with no shame.

Words For Thoughts

Why not pray when
Soul are crying out for faith
Hear the joy of thunder
Live not in tears for the multitude of questions
Hear the laughter
Be not in dark stains
Manifest history to light
See
The cauldren of hope and the laughter of truth
Hear the laughter
Why not pray
Capture the glory in faith
Hear the thoughts
Hear the laughter
How can you look for comfort?
When comfort is gazed in the kingdom of the Lord
Why not pray?

Heartless Soul

Anyone have pain killers for heartbreak?
Please feed thee
I'm in need of this indeed
Give me freedom so I can be
for I'm a fighter of this sickness of heart break
a world of loneliness parted by two
Who will save my heart when my soul is dead
Please oh please show me the pathway to one
I'm in need of this indeed
Please feed thee
Does anyone know where a broken heart goes to patch their hearts?
Why don't you give me the answer called hope?
Give me light called love
Give me song called free
Please oh please show me the pathway to one
Does anyone have a spare heart to I can borrow?
Please oh please save my soul from this darkness called sorrow
I'm in need of this indeed
Please feed thee
a new heart free from pain
a new heart free from hate
anyone have pain killers for heartbreak?

Liquid Thoughts

"Where is freedom?" an old man cries out
On the deck he stands
Folded arms and pose with curled up lips
Memory of ancient music echo through ships
A dark moon light balanced with wishes beneath
Slave whips
Worries stir with liquid thoughts
"Where is freedom,"
the old man asks "where may I find
Sea of moonlight free?,
There I will set my feet in to swing,
With ancient music echoing mellow notes
There I will go
I will breathe underneath
My ship to freedom"
the old man asks
"where is freedom?"
taken strokes of Liquid thoughts hasten down trouble throat
There he sits asking
himself
"where Is freedom?"
with folded arms and curled lips.

Dead Man Grave

Here they come walking stiff like mummies
1 by 1
2 by 2
Ghosts of dead men meet their faith where they lay
Undertaker walks by meeting husband and wife standing
Side by side
Unidentifiable sounds break, echoing past silent walls
1 by 1
2 by 2
There they fall through the grave, far yonder, there in the fields,
there goes another and another
provoking sounds of dead man grave
1 by 1
2 by 2
There they come through the gate
Dry tear awake with stirred ghosts
A rose drops
1 by 1
2 by 2
There they come walking stiff
Unconscious still meeting faith where it lies;
dead man grave
1 by 1
2 by 2

If Be

If she shall be the beloved friend,
Lord I pray to you beneath
Her star
For she is a lighting star that
I hope to light my dreams
If she shall be the beloved gift
Let her come as she will freely
With quiet eyes aglow
A character of a strong soul and will
Lord let her mind be clear
With wisdom and goals
If she shall be the beloved soul
Dear lord let the flames of life
Keep their flickers and burn with
Happiness and joy
If she shall be the beloved gift
I pray for her new found age
Come with laughter for her soul and love
If she shall be the beloved soul
I pray she'll be strong like an oak tree in mind
Lord I pray you see the greatness
in her eyes and kindness in her speech,
Let her soul hold truth for other to see
If she shall be the beloved gift

My Star

How I'm to exist without my star,
What have I done that is so evil to dim
my light that holds my night, shining Joy,
no more star in sight to shine my passion
I have become dark in my soul
Lost in time
Lost from my sight;
my star shines for another
This is by far my fear,
I see happiness only frown upon me
And joy itself has left me with only shame
My star
I hope and pray, knees shaking with pain
Before my prime gently walks away and welcomes
the future that is me as a gray headed old man
That I find a star that is bright, lovely and beautiful like you.

Honor

Her hope full of love as she wrote in a letter to her husband who was
sent to the war and said
"I shall with all willingness and duty to perform as you command."
She spoke with sorrow; pure sense of truth
"I'm altogether ignorant to the truth that I may find confessing
I keep all grace of imagination that your poor
mind and heart may hold upon me,
For I may be brighter to acknowledge, ignorant to fault
Do see my loyalty both in love and truth,
I show through my duty, and all in certainty affection.
You may find outside my grace to another subject of your fancy
I have followed you as your companion beyond your desire and I honor
you in your entire good name.
I shall never stain your name and worthiness with disloyal heart.
I shall keep true words with you
You shall see I have more firmness in my mind
I shall show you what makes love so sweet and yet so dangerous.
The reasons are permitted to form the union of our hearts to love and
love itself shall show extreme states of apathy and madness.
I shall with all willingness and duty to perform as you command."
A moment of imagination passes as her husband reads the letter. As
he was finishes, Tears provoke a smile in hope to see his wife.

Last Wisdom

Last moon I stretched her words and whisper in the dark silently.
There in the mist of the night
I saw silence betray me
Traveling away to spark a moment,
Last moon I stretched her words and whisper in the dark silently.
There she appears like a star on a journey, fresh and bright with a
White, golden mist of hair.
Her smile held the yoke of a daylight bright
Graceful touch brings outbust to memories of pride, strength and
perseverence.
She spoke gently in the midst of good judgement
Praise holds her wisdom.
Last moon, cells created by foul thoughts and unspoken
Bonds birth a new Self-determination.
All thoughts lay deaf as I wait for last moon to depart the whispers I
have giving to the dark silently.

Star

Pale eyes gone
The eyes of the dark will shine
the burning star
Pale eyes gone
The eyes light gave friendship
to
The broken heart
Pale eyes gone
left behind dreams of a hopeless path
pale eyes gone
darkness unable to break overwhelms light
pale eyes gone
the eyes of light give darkness a light to friendship.
Pale eyes gone.

Sallie

Have you seen Sallie?
dark wine eyes,
Brown sugar Sallie,
A new hope for the country
Carmel lips
Thick thighs marvelous
hips
Oh dear, a sweet heart with no fear
Coffee brown Sallie
Have you seen Sallie?
Plum chest sweet cherry
Peach shape sweetie
Oh Sallie
Peach blush sweet honey
Have you seen Sallie
A treat so sweet to the country?

Accident

A city of clouds approach the mid-night black
A shower of steam came where lovers and killers bond
Where hate and murders confine
a city of clouds brush its wings against the ungiven path
to find shame and joy to blame
there is an accident where sorrow cry and truth die
killers came to show honor
lovers hold, hand and hand, to walk in tribute
of truth death
steam of thought feed the mind and the mid-night black
became a whole to life accident

Innocent

What do you say to your dreams
When your mother and hero fall
What do your hopes become?
What would they find?
Who would they find
The unknown innocent eyes to fight
The mind with cotton sky or will,
Burning fingers hold the
Final, warmed against the wishes,
Of the falling stars?
What would dreams fight for ?
A night in freedoms smile
Or would dreams be left back like dry
dust that heros fall upon?
What do you say to your dreams
When your mother and hero fall?

Deal to Wrong

I have completed a great deal to wrong,
I'm demanding to do things right
Nevertheless the old wind is long gone
I try to exterminate what is already dead,
Wisdom from dead wiseman
continue to sit in silence
Misled troves on a cold morning,
I intone as I was the wind,
And smolder like the fire.
Trembling; cold frost lives in my heart,
For all the anger this came forth
racing my words.
They twine together as a whole,
however live together as two.
I have completed a great deal to wrong,
Now I'm demanding to do things right
Nevertheless the old wind is long gone
I try to exterminate what already dead
Roses that are ancient,
And my sea no longer blue, Once at peace,
hidden for undying boundaries
Will subsequently be.
The shock continues.
This life became a railway bridge not to be crossed.

Gloomy

Blank eyes sad expression
Blank soul gloomy depression
Striving to find this being
that I envision
It floods deep within
taking me like sin
Lost the cause without reason
affection without sense,
Insane became time without season.
Blank eyes sad expression
Blank soul gloomy depression
Facing life like a cancerous sore,
A foul bloodsucker that eats at my core.
Cold mist air, surrounded isolation
Living wasted
The contribution to me once bestowed.
A tribute and satisfaction now bereaved
Revealing impure delicate wings
A sorry night unborn sings
An unnoticed identity clouded
Lost my soul, the information unlisted
Lost in someone so bent and twisted
Blank eyes sad expression
Blank soul gloomy depression

Desert Rose

What become of the rose left undisturbed in the desert?
How can a rose escape?
In this world of cruel misery.
The poise of defeat,
the thoughts for all discovery firm to bear
Who has the care for the desert rose,
In this world of cruel miserey.
Heritage long gone ancient times,
What become of the rose left undisturbed in the desert?
How can a rose escape?
In this world of cruel misery.
Will there be a soul to water thoughts
For desert roses?
When will darkness fall to light.
Will we eventually find a way,
will angels tears dry, cold, with midnight frost?
What become of the rose left undisturbed in the desert?

Strength

I was waken to see the Lord this past evening
An event breaks my way
This event has something to say
How could I be so stubborn? To see the reason for one man
Lost in another lesson, for one eye open
gain of strength, another lay in death
Where will I be now?
Where will this light be now?
How dark thoughts bleed of truth?
Who will my hands holds as faith?
I was awaken to see the Lord this past evening
A voice echoes my name
I was in fear forever my heart holds no shame
I try to find the meaning, in return find me
Where will I be now?
Where will this light be now?
When this voice crys my name I plunge apart
I saw the words connecting in line with my heart
I saw beauty leave grace
I was too afraid to steal a glance

Why was this event sent to break my way?
I'm lost with oh so much to say
Where will I be now?
Where will this light be now?
I have lost the reasons
I have trird to gain lost questions
How could I gain this passion?
Oh, oh how will this be my lesson?
I was awaken to see the Lord this past last evening
An event breaks my way
Where will I be now ?
Oh Lord, this is my song, I cry to you now?
Hope you see my call now.

Inferno

The sun burnt the forest
Fields became seas of inferno
lost soul's painted red fortune
as waves bended in and a tide's
dark mist,
came along with rainbows under the daylight
while
voices of fathers resounded in lost intellect
Collect not their worries,
their love, nor the dark that awaits
Moreover, the inferno set in their eyes
Sorrow walks along the ways of the dry land
Sadness sits to wait in peace
and
stares of the fortunate freeze the dark,
buring forest glows with crystal blue
forever be a glow of peace
Love and humanity
Forever deceased.

Hate

Rage flashes heat
frustration frowns
as
Intentsitity builds
Intelligent, lost directions and reasons
Secret lies break, the hidden promise
finds the truth.
Unfaithful heart
Un-embrace discover
Long gone the dreams
Judgement tasted a
Familiar purpose
where rage organized flashing heat
Frustration frowns
as
intentity builds.

No to Truth

Underneath the belly of deceit
Love suffers and satisfaction overtakes a new conquest
Stirred up anger fuels lust
Underneath the lie's, crushed by warmth.
ungratefulness,
judgements,
all became playful to touch
values of truth pass silently like mist in the darkest night
laws, on no account, found justice
love came with unspoken treats,
Screaming, betrayed by two, suffered by four.
Young love stands gallantly with shaking hands
As,
Blind thoughts, unwholesome stumbles on
no confession.
Love
Falls with gloomy desert
sitting underneath the belly of deceit
Satisfaction overtakes a new conquest
Stirred up anger fuels lust
Underneath the lie's, crushed by warmth.

I Know Love

I have known love
Ancient as the world
Both young and old
I know love
I have seen love, like freedom to a slave
Like wings to a dove
Like affection to the heart or like tenderness to the body
I have known love like prayers to the soul,
like love be to God be the love to my whole
I have known love and seen love stare deep
in the eyes of the hopeless and win courage
I have seen love, counterfeit and genuine,
I have known love
seen love both irreplaceable like a kiss on the cheek
like a marrage that never lasts
I bring forth faith and truth
ancients young and old
I know love
I have known love, antique to my eyes
have you seen love?
I know love
I have known love
Ancient as the world
Both young and old
I know love
yet I have not found love.

Glory Be To Man

Come to thee my son
Be not on knees and hands
for glory
Be for man and man be to God
Stand upon your feet for love is true, strong like prayers
Hold truth not lies nor fate, move forth onto thee
Create levels that are higher, brighter never dim, keep
Eyes never astray, awake for love thee shall be
See deep in both love and truth, for sour heart may
Echo for it
Keep souls awaken
for
there, in life, are mountains harder
never shall you
Be upon your knees,
for glory be to man, truth and love be to God.

Smiling

I stop seeing what became of today
seek only the touch of yestaday
What have I seen, and hold in my mind has gone tomorrow
I have seen foolishness, came with tears to call for smiles in sorrow
I'm gone, provoked by something new, that of which I wish to borrow
Who to call or ask when gloomy clouds undone
I'm sure there will be something of a smile to greet me
I hope no future sees me weakened or shamed
when I come to see the light of love
for there is no sweeter sight to gaze upon as one with a dove
for it has shows me the way,
I will endure the darkness for it shows me the stars
And yet endure the visions that are far
I see that I smile in the warranty of freedom
Nontheless seek a path to be in the kingdom
I see and ask myself what went wrong
To this life's beats created by crys to a song
I try the truth that I thought
will become my strength
I stop smiling to see the root of man's reach
I took a journey in my past to see only
My weakness smiling at me
A white shining stare of a defeat
I stop smiling
I took a wink in todays eyes
I realized the stories are released by untold lies that lay at ease
I start smiling.

Words Holding

Don't I wish I could write or
play a song for you?
A song that is playful like a child
Save for yet true
I would never snub the feelings or provoke the music
Although, I mend those broken written pages,
give presents to future for time and ages
Painting a four walled box trapped inside
by humanity theme and wages
Don't I wish I could write or
play a song for you?
Foretells the future a given life to tears
the past is at its core stirring all those years
deep inside
like an ocean tide
it just keeps undulating
Living scared or sore burning
Don't I wish I could write or
play a song for you?

There's a rhythm inside me
That's constantly leading me to see
to your musical being
No I don't really sing
To mend my trouble pains
But your words ran through my soul and my veins
and it remains baiting
Don't I wish I could write or
play a song for you?
When I think of you
I wish I could . . .
Don't you wish I would
play a song for you
when I gaze into your eyes I see
that your words holding a song and rhythm for me.
Don't I wish I could write or
play a song for you?.

Dry Your Eyes

Glory has come
Since the beginning of time we cry without hope
Terrible with storms of war
Dry your eyes
We are the North Star that shines with reflections of our mother's laughter and images of her joy
The silence of the horizon rejoices with shades that is awaken in our smiles
We are fighters of life's burning sun and now we gain the ownership of our freedom
Dry your eyes
The journey is not yet finished
The wings of our father's hopes we carry, with the heritage of their forefathers
You must know we are watched in the wisdom of poets and champions.
Dry your eyes
On this day the heart of time has hailed; it arms stretched with the length of hope and faith to embrace the daybreak.
The greatest rivers have given their peace to bond with the fisherman
For today is the day we eat full and enjoying this marvelous day,
Today we shine with time and history has become our truth
Dry your eyes
Glory has come.

To My Knees

I once fell upon my knees
They gave way beneath me
And down I went
Just like the movies
The weight of loving and losing
So great
I could no longer hold my own
and I would fall
Hands turned to the sky
To my knees
Loving you
Losing you
And moving on
Like the movies
All drama and tragedy,
I am a lamenting Christ
Asking why
I fall, face first into the grass
No pain just
The soft clean smell of spring's children pushing
Toward the sky. In my nostrils
I breathe in and out so hard

That all I could see, smell and taste was new green grass
Loving you
Losing you
And moving on
Like the movies
All drama and tragedy
I know my sacrifice will, in the end,
Buy a cosmic cure for someone somewhere. And now: I move on,
Into this lullaby of a future.
I still smell the grass
I still see the robin's as they returns in the spring
But with each passing day I hope love keeps you home on winter's nights,
folded between blankets and contented slumber. And forget what went before
I used to fall to my knees.

Summer Love

charming frame
beauty stimulating senses
White flowery dress,
exquisite smile
beautiful eyes refleting the even sky.
Stand out figure
Greacfuly pressed against the background
Thought blessed by journey
presences of fantasies
Admire by appeareance
Amazed by tender touch
Smooth delicate lips,
Betraying thoughts came incarcerated by perfume,
Love and lust melt on the body, like a candle in the dark
Impulsive visions expand out lost
Gracious sensitive embrace
Cold heart gives in
small amount of friendship permited
appears a greater effect of admitation
waiting to decide upon a verdict tenderly.

Divine

When the thoughts no longer bring consecrate upon me
My poetry writes her name,
I give in and let it be
Her love and beauty became my fame
So she came to me,
her smile gives reason for my satisfaction
I hum lessons of dying pain
She give me facts and her visions became my undying passion
Imagination brings forth relief washing down the drain
Divine she has become
For my heart holds faith sweeter than a kiss
Amazing she came to me
I see truth never amiss.

Lie's

Promises lay with lilly's
Cold shivering
simple thoughts take relief to play wildly with worthless conscious
Late night lies feel free to innocent dreams
Prayer from cold lips left
Truth gives birth to an apology for wrongs,
duration holds in memory
Photos of mistrust came to lie beside promise's
Lies dance astray
Promise set to play truth
late night lies and misunderstandings.

The Rebirth of Africa

Today the seed of a new era has been planted
We have come from the dying path,
The length of history from fear of iniquity
The indecency of our motherland shows us we are not afraid of the future, for it brings growth and joy in her mother heart.
We now know the seed of immorality that once grew in our father's farm will not see a day in light
We hold the truths which will guide up to more equal motions, our brother's and sister's in Darfur and those whose blood was shed in ravages of war, we are here to give rebirth to their souls and make certain their life did not rot in vain.
We will stand; feet strong as Africa, ready to take on the responsibilities of this journey
For we know where there is life there shall be achievement that will leave the dead with pride that their hard work we did not forsake.
We have watched; our hands away from the darkness that we have seen, and shown no growth known to our path
We demand the glow of our forefather's wisdom to brighten our future which holds our liberty
We come across hope with a vision that the invisible is and holds elements to our life and destiny.

We believe in the truth by pushing the limit we can only find the adventure that we can claim as our victory
Today we discover the root that holds our people proud and the values and responsibilities instilled in us that their sons and daughters have not dared to waste the fruitfulness of the tree that gave us life.
We as people have come together to know no matter the hardship we face if there is chance there is away, to look in the eyes of truth and trust that we Africans will show our beauty, our voice, our sense of caring and our culture to the earth and its people
So come let us wash our hands in life's basin and hope again
For this is the truth as a testimony to the rebirth of Africa.
Welcome to the rebirth of Africa.

Unselfish

Too long his heart has been in the bags of suspense
impossible for him not to admire in her sensiblities
honor her by judgment
A cheerful heart he wished for her to contain,
for one quality to a strong mind
Yet entertained all sentiment beyond
that of his own immediate pleasure
A thread to hold such suspense at length became a habit
A frame which holds delusion found unwritten courage
an image blended with ideas of twisted thoughts
ideas condensed the records of his lonly heart
beatings with sprits unknown to the purity of his soul.
There he finds expectation to fill his gloomy solitude
with delightful nightmares
yet he nursed the truth in his reality of affection to offend the
ears of selfish sensibility.

Photograph

lost memories
A broken heart
A hanging shelf filled with arctic memories
I stroll lonely through fate
stroll upon love
I find a path nowhere to go,
drgan still sustain
Aturning memories sit still framed in my heart
lesson thoughts refuse to learn
I stumble in a photograph
Dust grabs my intrest by the neck
My heart calls no question
lost memories
A broken heart
Beside me shadows stand as my soul
Another breaking point
Direction lost in my mind
Unpredictable Journey found in my heart
Tattoos, photographs blemish
Strolling truth stand on trial
For what? I came to boast
lost thoughts nowhere to go
lost memories
A broken heart

The Dream

On the day she took my virginity
Her smile was oh so beauiful
Oh so tempting
I stood there trembling with fear
As I lived my wildest dreams
She touched me with her light
And I let her see my words in the dark
She called my name like a drum that beat our motions wild
My mind was overtaken with a feeling, I reached deep deep into
Her thoughts
She brings shivers down my soul
My hands sweep across
I let my fingers caress the darkness
However, I find nothing but air
My words became her light
So I reached the end of her pleasuring road
Nothing moves me more than her sweet voice
Nothing I know leaves me sweating tired and satisfied
She asked me for an encore so I give her what she asked for
I give and give and give and I give a little more
Till she cried out "No More"
From then on I knew I what I had become;
I'm an artist on stage.

Poetry

If poetry was a woman she would be a fantasy of
imaginative experience by impossible definition
Her lips will quiver with sun light kisses that can only give birth to daylight
if ever her thoughts give lesson to ignorant and paths to the lonesome child
Her fingers will hold the truth of satifaction
Her movement of caring could be expressed mainly
with emotions of matters and rhythmic
Never the cause of attendant or servant.
Her smile resolves determination and strength to play languages of
evocation and romantic responses
If poetry was a woman
Her characters will be named synonyms and antoynms for they both
hold truth and are
erroneous.
If poetry was a woman our tonuges will speak to her body with
language such as this.
If poetry was a woman she would be a fantasy of
imaginative experience by impossible definition.

Smile, someone is thinking about you
"Is that so? Well if it true I will smile with my heart,
and hope will glow on my face."

> Desert Rose
> Don't you worry, don't be lonely
> Heaven knows, Heaven knows
> in a dry and weary land a flower grows
> His desert rose.
> —White Heart—"Desert Rose"

Get Published, Inc!
Thorofare, NJ 08086
19 November 2009
BA2009262